## Cause and Effect

# Into THE WEST

**CAUSES AND EFFECTS**

of U.S. Westward Expansion

### BY TERRY COLLINS

Consultant:
Malcolm J. Rohrbough
Professor Emeritus
Department of History
The University of Iowa

CAPSTONE PRESS
a capstone imprint

W9-BKE-841

Fact Finders Books are published by Capstone Press,
1710 Roe Crest Drive, North Mankato, Minnesota 56003
www.capstonepub.com

**Library of Congress Cataloging-in-Publication Data**
Collins, Terry (Terry Lee)
Into the west : causes and effects of U.S. westward expansion / by Terry Collins.
pages cm.—(Fact finders. Cause and effect)
Includes bibliographical references and index.
Summary: "Explains westward expansion in the United States and its impact"—
Provided by publisher.
ISBN 978-1-4765-0237-3 (library binding)—ISBN 978-1-4765-3403-9 (pbk.)—
ISBN 978-1-4765-3411-4 (ebook pdf)
1. United States—Territorial expansion—Juvenile literature. 2. West (U.S.)—History—
Juvenile literature. 3. West (U.S.)—Discovery and exploration—Juvenile literature. I.
Title. II. Title: Causes and effects of U.S. westward expansion.
E179.5.C55 2014
978—dc23                                                     2013001644

**Editorial Credits**
Jennifer Besel, editor; Alison Thiele, designer; Svetlana Zhurkin, media researcher;
    Laura Manthe, production specialist

**Photo Credits**
Alamy: North Wind Picture Archives, 15; Courtesy Scotts Bluff National Monument,
cover (middle), 5; Dreamstime: Dana Kenneth Johnson, 13; iStockphotos:
HultonArchive, 18, stocksnapper, 14; Library of Congress, 4, 8, 9, 11, 16, 27, 28, 29;
Newscom: akg-images, 22, Design Pics, 24, Picture History, 23; Shutterstock: Antonio
Abrignani, 21, kovacsf, 25, Ronald Sumners, cover (inset)

Printed in the United States of America in North Mankato, Minnesota.
032016 009601R

# Table OF CONTENTS

# Spreading WEST

Before the 1800s the United States was a small country. People lived, worked, and played in states east of the Mississippi River. Across the river was an unknown frontier. Fur trappers and traders, American Indians, and a few explorers had traveled across the rough land. But most people had no idea what this western land was like.

All that changed in the 1800s. Families began moving westward to start farms. Brave men crossed the rough mountains in search of gold. The phrase "Go west, young man" became a common saying for anyone looking for a fresh start.

American Indians and fur trappers lived off the land in the unknown western territory.

Thousands of people went west in the 1800s, looking to start new lives.

But what caused this great movement west? And how did westward expansion affect the United States? Several factors made people want to risk their savings and their lives to move west. And their movement changed the country forever.

# What Caused WESTWARD EXPANSION?

America's expansion into the West took many years. But it all started with one big purchase.

## Cause #1—The Louisiana Purchase

In 1803 President Thomas Jefferson offered to buy the **port** of New Orleans from the French for $10 million. French leader Napoleon Bonaparte took the deal. In fact, he said if Jefferson threw in an extra $5 million, the United States could buy the entire Louisiana Territory. So in October 1803, the United States purchased 828,000 square miles (2,144,510 square kilometers) of land. The country's size doubled overnight.

**port:** a harbor or place where boats and ships can dock or anchor safely

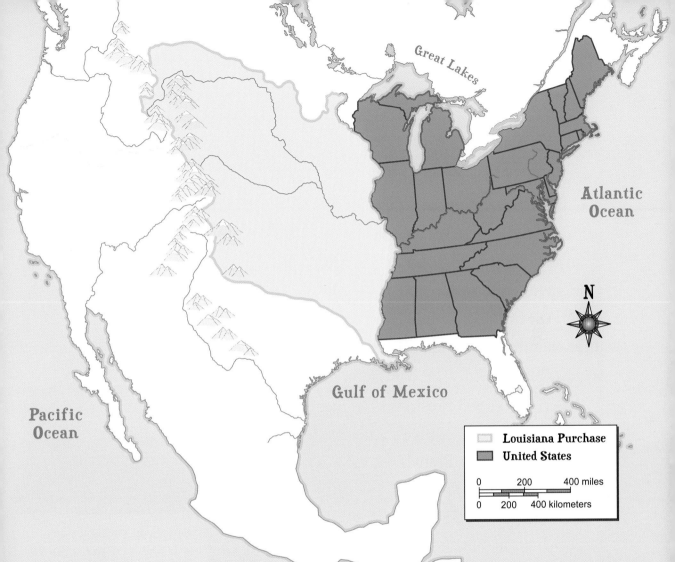

Great Lakes

Atlantic
Ocean

N

Gulf of Mexico

Pacific
Ocean

☐ Louisiana Purchase
■ United States

0        200        400 miles
0     200     400 kilometers

Wanting to know more about the unexplored territory, the president set up the Corps of Discovery. Led by army officers Meriwether Lewis and William Clark, the group explored the United States' new land. The explorers filled notebooks with information on plants, animals, and American Indians. They also discovered a land route to the Pacific Ocean.

## Cause #2—Manifest Destiny

Lewis and Clark drew about 140 maps showing the way west. People began to use those maps to follow in the group's footsteps. The growing desire for people to go west became known as America's "**Manifest Destiny**."

The phrase "Manifest Destiny" became a popular term in the 1840s and 1850s. People began to believe it was the country's mission to grow in size and **influence**. They believed God gave white Americans the right to claim land, even if American Indians already lived there. People said that only after claiming the lands from the East Coast to the West would their "destiny" be complete.

Americans believed it was their destiny to move west. Here an artist drew "destiny" in the form of a woman leading travelers.

**Manifest Destiny:** the belief that God gave white Americans the right to take over lands that belonged to other people

**influence:** to have an effect on someone or something

Miners looked for gold in cool mountain streams.

## Cause #3—California Gold Rush

Just as Manifest Destiny was heating up, another major event got people moving. In 1848 gold was discovered in California. With dreams of big money, thousands of men headed to California. The Gold Rush saw about 300,000 treasure-hunters go west. Once in California, these gold-rushers stayed. Towns grew up around them and populations boomed.

**FAST FACT:** The phrase "strike it rich" came from the California Gold Rush. Miners hoped to strike a piece of gold to make their fortunes.

## Cause #4–The Homestead Act

In 1846 the United States went to war with Mexico. At the end of the Mexican War in 1848, the United States gained another 1 million square miles (2,590,000 square km) of land. With this new addition, the U.S. government owned a lot of western lands. But leaders could not agree on how to let citizens buy the land.

In 1860 Abraham Lincoln was elected president. Southern states believed he would end slavery. By June 1861, 11 states had left the union. The United States was in a civil war. The U.S. government continued to create laws throughout the war. Without leaders from those 11 states, Congress passed the **Homestead** Act in 1862. This new law allowed citizens to have up to 160 acres (65 hectares) of land. In exchange, the people agreed to live on the land for five years. They had to raise crops and build a house. Millions of people took advantage of this opportunity to become landowners.

**FAST FACT:** The Homestead Act said people who had "borne arms against the U.S. government" could not get these lands. So anyone who fought for the South during the Civil War could not get land.

**homestead:** a piece of land with room for a new home and farm
**transcontinental:** crossing a continent

## Cause #5—The Transcontinental Railroad

The **Transcontinental** Railroad opened the West to all. No longer did travelers have to tackle dangerous routes with oxen and wagon. Travel time was cut from months to just days. Built between 1863 and 1869, the Transcontinental Railroad joined the United States from coast to coast. Goods could be shipped quickly and cheaply. New towns and factories began to appear along the railroad routes. Where the railroads were built, people followed.

# The VOYAGE WEST

For the early pioneers, traveling west was difficult. After Lewis and Clark explored the Louisiana Territory, hunters and trappers were the first to follow in their footsteps. These rugged men also started blazing new routes to the West. These early routes were by water, up the Missouri River into the Rocky Mountains.

By the mid-1830s, new land routes made it possible for families to go in wagons. These routes weren't easy to travel though. Rugged dirt paths, mountain passes, and rushing rivers made the trip difficult. But with each passing year, settlers expanded what became known as the Oregon Trail.

The starting point for the Oregon Trail was Independence, Missouri. Independence had a large trading post where travelers could get supplies for the long trip. By mid-April each year, hundreds of wagons lined the town. Mid-April was the best time to leave because travelers would be able to cross mountain ranges before the freezing winter months.

a typical wagon used on the Oregon Trail

wagon bow

bonnet

sideboards

jockey box

yankee bed

iron tire

doubletree

singletree

brake block

hub

felly rim

axle

falling tongue

People did not travel quickly on the Oregon Trail. Oxen were not known for their speed. On a good day, they could pull the wagon about 15 miles (24 km). Oxen also had to be led by a man on foot.

Travel by wagon was not cheap either. The wagon itself could cost about $400—a fortune at that time. Supplies for a family of four to make the six-month trip were also expensive. A typical shopping list included:

- 800 pounds (363 kilograms) of flour
- 200 pounds (91 kg) of lard
- 700 pounds (318 kg) of bacon
- 100 pounds (45 kg) of fruit
- 75 pounds (34 kg) of coffee
- 25 pounds (11 kg) of salt

Travelers brought everything they expected to need on the journey. There were a few outposts along the trail. But they were hundreds of miles apart.

Men loaded their wagons before the long journey.

# The Donner Party

In 1846 a group of 89 people, now known as the Donner Party, headed to California. The Donner Party left late and did not travel the Oregon Trail. Instead they took a short cut that would take 400 miles (644 km) off the 2,500-mile (4,000-km) trip.

But it was no shortcut. The new path trapped the travelers in the Sierra Nevada Mountains. Bad weather kept the Donner Party stuck in the mountains for months. When food ran out, the travelers were forced to eat the frozen flesh of members who had died. When they were finally rescued, only 48 members were still alive.

Crossing the Rocky Mountains was a difficult and deadly part of the Oregon Trail.

The Oregon Trail crossed the Rocky Mountains to the valleys of what would become the state of Oregon. Roughly one out of 17 travelers died along the way. Cholera was the number one killer. Cholera caused diarrhea and severe dehydration. A sufferer's entire body shut down because of lack of water.

**cholera:** a dangerous disease that causes severe sickness and diarrhea

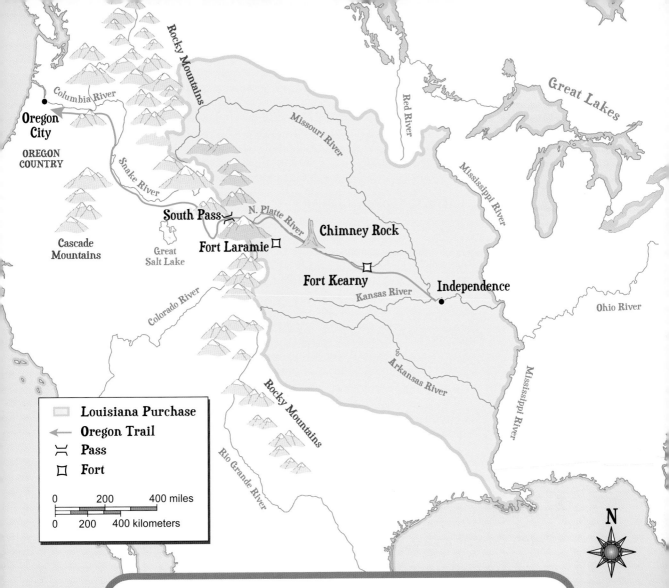

Oregon City was the destination for most trail travelers. Families rested in town, then established their land claims in the region. The city grew quickly as settlers opened shops. The stores supplied new arrivals with materials to begin their new farms. The Columbia River provided water power for mills and factories to serve the growing population.

Mining camps were rugged places.

## There's Gold in Them Hills!

On January 24, 1848, James Marshall discovered gold in Coloma, California. A year later, California was swarming with miners hoping to strike it rich. As the news spread, the United States caught a case of "gold fever." Newspapers ran headlines about the fortune awaiting those brave enough to go west.

The Gold Rush really took off in 1849. Those who went west for gold were nicknamed the "Forty-niners" (49ers). Many of the 49ers used the Oregon Trail. But others traveled from the East Coast to the West by ship. The 49ers were almost all men. They left their families behind to go in search of fortune. Wives and children kept the homes running, waiting for word from their husbands and fathers.

People came from all over the world to find their fortunes in California. At least 100,000 people flocked to the area in just two years. All these people pushed American Indians off their lands, forcing them to find new places to live.

For most 49ers, the dream of fortune never came true. Many had trouble even making enough money to survive. The life of a miner was difficult. Miners spent 10 hours a day **panning** for gold. After a long day, they went back to their camps. Miners lived near each other in shacks built from scraps of wood, logs, and canvas. Mice and lice were common in these horrible homes.

Soon some of the camps grew into mining towns. Stores, saloons, and other businesses opened up. In town, miners often gambled away the little bits of gold they did find.

**pan:** to sift sand in a pan of water in search of gold

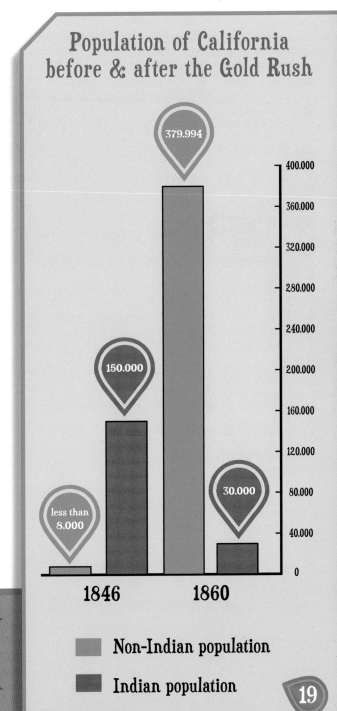

Population of California before & after the Gold Rush

379.994

150.000

30.000

less than 8.000

1846     1860

400.000
360.000
320.000
280.000
240.000
200.000
160.000
120.000
80.000
40.000
0

Non-Indian population

Indian population

## Home Sweet Home

During and after the Civil War, an estimated 270 million acres (110 million hectares) were claimed and settled under the Homestead Act. Getting the land was easy. Keeping it was the hard part.

Life as a homesteader was difficult. By the 1860s, settlement had moved onto the **Great Plains**. The open plains offered few trees for wood or shelter. Natural disasters such as freezing winters and high winds could wreck a small farm's crop. Raising livestock was also hard since little natural grass grew for cattle to eat. Loneliness without neighbors and the stress of constant work caused many homesteaders to give up and leave their claims.

But for many, the opportunity to own land was too important to give up. Each family member was expected to help. Men plowed the fields, planted crops, and harvested them. Women handled all the cooking, cleaning, sewing, and childcare. They also took care of the family's vegetable garden. Children worked too. They helped in the fields or with household chores. They also collected buffalo or cow chips to burn for heat.

**Great Plains:** the broad, level land that stretches through the middle of the United States

Early homesteaders worked day and night to build a life on the Plains.

## Choo Choo!

The railroad made a big change in the lives of homesteaders. No longer were they out on the prairie all alone. The railroad brought goods, such as cloth, sugar, and coffee. It carried newspapers filled with updates about the rest of the world.

But like everything else about the West, building the rail wasn't easy. To build the Transcontinental Railroad workers had to lay tracks over land that rose up to 7,000 feet (2,134 m) in the Sierra Nevada Mountains. They had to use explosives to blast tunnels through the mountains.

Finding workers to build the railroad was difficult too. Much of the work was done by Chinese laborers. The Chinese originally came to America seeking gold. But when the mines didn't work out, they had to find other work. Up to 15,000 Chinese worked on the railroad.

# What Effects Did WESTWARD EXPANSION HAVE?

The movement of so many people to the West had deep and lasting effects.

## Effect #1—A Changed Economy

The Transcontinental Railroad changed the country's **economy**. Businesses now sold products to people hundreds of miles away. New towns and factories began to appear along the railroad routes. The Transcontinental Railroad was key in joining all parts of the United States together as one country.

**economy:** the ways in which a country handles its money and resources

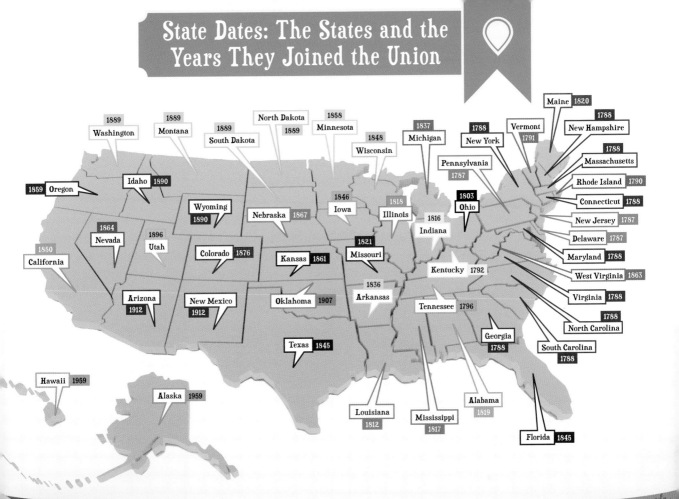

# State Dates: The States and the Years They Joined the Union

Maine 1820
Vermont 1791
New Hampshire 1788
New York 1788
Massachusetts 1788
Washington 1889
Montana 1889
North Dakota 1889
Minnesota 1858
Michigan 1837
Pennsylvania 1787
Rhode Island 1790
South Dakota 1889
Wisconsin 1848
Connecticut 1788
Oregon 1859
Idaho 1890
Ohio 1803
New Jersey 1787
Delaware 1787
Wyoming 1890
Iowa 1846
Illinois 1818
Indiana 1816
Maryland 1788
Nebraska 1867
West Virginia 1863
Nevada 1864
Utah 1896
Kentucky 1792
Virginia 1788
California 1850
Colorado 1876
Kansas 1861
Missouri 1821
North Carolina 1788
Arizona 1912
New Mexico 1912
Oklahoma 1907
Arkansas 1836
Tennessee 1796
Georgia 1788
South Carolina 1788
Texas 1845
Hawaii 1959
Alaska 1959
Louisiana 1812
Mississippi 1817
Alabama 1819
Florida 1845

## Effect #2—Growth

The long term effects of westward expansion can also be seen by simply looking at the growth of the United States. Thirteen colonies grew into 48 states by 1912. Two more were added by 1960. Westward expansion is responsible for making the United States one of the largest countries in the world.

# Effect #3—A Changed Way of Life

Westward expansion had some negative effects too. American Indian tribes had lived on western lands for thousands of years. But contact with white explorers, settlers, and soldiers changed everything for American Indians.

White settlers received land through the Homestead Act. But that land was where American Indians had lived and hunted for centuries. Tribes were forced to move away from their homes.

Settlers and explorers also carried diseases such as smallpox. The American Indians had never come in contact with those diseases. Their bodies had no way to fight them off. Many American Indians died.

Ultimately, a way of life was lost. Because of westward expansion, the roaming lifestyle of the Plains Indians vanished. The U.S. government created **reservations** and forced tribes onto them. Defeated and beaten down, American Indians had no choice but to leave their homes.

**reservation:** an area of land set aside by the U.S. government for American Indians

Thousands of American Indians were forced to live on reservations far from their homelands.

# Major Fighting

The U.S. government made many promises to American Indian tribes about keeping their lands. But time and again the government broke those promises as more people moved west. Fights between government forces and Indian tribes were common as Americans expanded into the West.

One of the most famous conflicts took place in June 1876. The Battle of Little Bighorn was a two-day bloodbath. Colonel George Custer and the U.S. Seventh Calvary were wiped out by Sioux forces. But that "victory" did not stop westward expansion, and it could not save the Sioux's homeland.

## Effect #4—Looking at Slavery

Westward expansion forced the United States to look at the issue of slavery too. People were deeply divided on the issue. The southern states' economy depended on slave labor to run their large plantations. Many northern states had banned slavery. Before the mass movement west, there was an even balance of slave states and free states. But as people moved west, they wanted to make new states. Government leaders had to decide if slavery would be allowed in the new states.

Tempers flared and anger bubbled over. People on both sides of the issue were willing to fight for their beliefs. And that's exactly what they did. Leaders in Congress tried to compromise. But eventually 11 states left the union, and the U.S. Civil War began.

Westward expansion didn't directly cause the Civil War. But it did force the nation to make a decision on slavery. With the end of the war, slavery became illegal in all states.

Leaders in Congress angrily debated if states in the West should allow slavery.

Some people wanted to bring slaves with them as they moved west. Others wanted slavery banned. The differing opinions deeply divided the country.

## Cause and Effect

Much of what the United States is today was caused by westward expansion. It changed where and how people lived. It changed trade, travel, and business throughout the country. The effects of this movement—good and bad—still affect people today.

# GLOSSARY

**cholera** (KAH-luhr-uh)—a dangerous disease that causes severe sickness and diarrhea

**economy** (i-KAH-nuh-mee)—the ways in which a country handles its money and resources

**Great Plains** (GRAYT PLANES)—the broad, level land that stretches eastward from the base of the Rocky Mountains for about 400 miles (644 km) in the United States and Canada

**homestead** (HOHM-sted)—a piece of land with room for a new home and farm

**influence** (IN-floo-uhnss)—to have an effect on someone or something

**Manifest Destiny** (MAN-uh-fest DESS-tuh-nee)—the belief that God gave white Americans the right to take over lands that belonged to other people

**pan** (PAN)—to sift sand in a pan of water in search of gold

**port** (PORT)—a harbor or place where boats and ships can dock or anchor safely

**reservation** (rez-er-VAY-shuhn)—an area of land set aside by the U.S. government for American Indians

**transcontinental** (transs-kon-tuh-NEN-tuhl)—crossing a continent

# READ MORE

**Domnauer, Teresa**. *Westward Expansion*. A True Book. New York: Children's Press, 2010.

**Hinton, KaaVonia**. *To Preserve the Union: Causes and Effects of the Missouri Compromise*. Cause and Effect. North Mankato, Minn.: Capstone Press, 2014.

**Roza, Greg**. *Westward Expansion*. The Story of America. New York: Gareth Stevens Pub., 2011.

# INTERNET SITES

FactHound offers a safe, fun way to find Internet sites related to this book. All of the sites on FactHound have been researched by our staff.

Here's all you do:

Visit *www.facthound.com*

Type in this code: 9781476502373

Super-cool stuff! Check out projects, games and lots more at **www.capstonekids.com**

# CRITICAL THINKING USING THE COMMON CORE

1. What does *Manifest Destiny* mean? How was the phrase and belief behind it used to justify pushing American Indians off their lands? (Key Ideas and Details)

2. More than 300,000 people moved to California during the Gold Rush. How might the United States be different if gold had never been discovered there? Support your answer. (Integration of Knowledge and Ideas)

3. What new information can you gather by comparing the map on page 7 to the map on page 25? (Craft and Structure)

# INDEX